Carol
TO

Dee
FROM

Feb. 21, 2000
DATE

LITTLE ONES
C O L L E C T I O N

LITTLE TOUCHES OF GOD'S LOVE

Photography © 1998 by Virginia Dixon

Text copyright © 1998 by Garborg's, Inc.

Design by Thurber Creative

Published by Garborg's, Inc.
P. O. Box 20132, Bloomington, MN 55420

ISBN 1-881830-764

Printed in Hong Kong

Little Touches of God's Love

We have been in God's thought from all eternity, and in His creative love, His attention never leaves us.

MICHAEL QUOIST

God loves each one of us as if there were only one of us.

AUGUSTINE

He paints the lily of the field,
Perfumes each lily bell;
If He so loves the little flowers,
I know He loves me well.

MARIA STRAUS

I asked God for all things
that I might enjoy life.
He gave me life
that I might enjoy all things.

My friend
shall forever
be my friend,
and reflect
a ray of God
to me.

THOREAU

May God send His love like sunshine
in His warm and gentle way,
To fill each corner of your heart
each moment of today.

He surrounds me with lovingkindness
and tender mercies. He fills my
life with good things.

PSALM 103:4-5 TLB

God's fingers can touch nothing
but to mold it into loveliness.

GEORGE MACDONALD

Into all our lives, in many simple,
familiar ways, God infuses an element
of joy from the surprises of life,
which unexpectedly brighten our days
and fill our eyes with light.

LONGFELLOW

May you wake
each day with
His blessings and
sleep each night
in *His* keeping.

Faith makes
all things possible.
Hope makes
all things bright.
Love makes
all things easy.

God knows the
rhythm of my
spirit and knows
my heart thoughts.
He is as close
as breathing.

How precious it is, Lord, to realize that you are thinking about me constantly! I can't even count how many times a day your thoughts turn towards me.

PSALM 139:17 TLB

God loves and cares for us, even to the least event and smallest need of life.

HENRY EDWARD MANNING

Blue skies with white clouds on
summer days.... Tulips and roses and
violets and dandelions and daisies....
See how He loves us!

ALICE CHAPIN

May you be ever present
in the garden of His love.

You are...infinitely dear to the
Father, unspeakably precious to
Him. You are never, not
for one second, alone.

NORMAN DOWTY

Each day of life is a precious
gift from God.

Love is the sweet, tender, melting nature of God flowing from His heart.

The earth is filled with his tender love.

PSALM 33:5 TLB

Everything around me may change,
but our God is changeless!

CAROL KENT

God will never let you be shaken
or moved from your place
near His heart.

JONI EARECKSON TADA

All the things
in this world
are gifts and
signs of God's
love to us.

PETER KREEFT

The light of God surrounds me,
The love of God enfolds me,
The presence of God protects me,
God is always with me.